Ecosystems of North America

The Eastern Forest

Eileen Fielding

Benchmark Books

MARSHALL CAVENDISH
NEW YORK

Consultant: Richard Haley, Director, Goodwin Conservation Center

Benchmark Books
Marshall Cavendish Corporation
99 White Plains Road
Tarrytown, New York 10591-9001

Library of Congress Cataloging-in-Publication Data

Fielding, Eileen.
    The eastern forest / Eileen Fielding.
        p.   cm.—(Ecosystems of North America)
    Includes bibliographical references (p.   ) and index.
    Summary: Examines the forests of eastern North America, their ecosystems, and their responses to temperature and weather.
    ISBN 0-7614-0895-9 (lib. bdg.)
    1. Forest ecology—East (U.S.)—Juvenile literature. 2. Forest ecology—Canada, Eastern—Juvenile literature. [1. Forest ecology.] I. Title II. Series.
QH104.5.E37F54   97 33115
577.3'0974—c21   CIP
                                                                            AC

Photo Credits

The photographs in this book are used by permission and through the courtesy of:
Animals Animals/Earth Scenes: Alan G. Nelson 9; Maresa Pryor 19; Leonard Lee Roe III 21; Philip Hart 24; Patti Murray 40; Zig Leszczynski 44-45; Bates Littlehales 48 (top/bottom); C.W. Schwartz 51 (middle); Linda E. Bailey, back cover. *Peter Arnold, Inc:* Jean F. Stoick 6; Werner H. Müller 22-23; S.J. Krasemann 26, 47; Fritz Pölkina 32; Jim Wark 36-37; Steve Kaufman 39; David Cavagnaro 47 (inset); Martha Cooper 58. *Photo Researchers, Inc:* L. Brun 4-5; Alvin E. Staffan 18; Jeff Lepore cover, 28; John Bova 30-31; A.L. Parnes 34 (inset); Gregory K. Scott 35; Tom & Pat Leeson 38 (top); George Kleiman 42; Harry Engels 42 (inset); Porterfield/Chickering 43; Kenneth Murray 46; Tim Davis 52; G. Carleton Ray 54-55; Will & Deni McIntyre 57 (top). *Tom Stack & Associates:* Diana L. Stratton 25. *Visuals Unlimited:* Glenn Oliver 16-17; Bruce Gaylord 33; Richard Thom 34. Cover design by Ann Antoshak for BBI.

Series Created and Produced by BOOK BUILDERS INCORPORATED

Printed in Hong Kong

Contents

Exploring the Eastern Forest

The Eastern Forest spreads from Canada to Florida and from the Mississippi River to the Atlantic Ocean. Take a moment to imagine yourself in this forest. Are you forming a picture of trees? Trees are important in a forest, but they are only part of the picture. An explorer could spend a lifetime learning about the Eastern Forest. There are so many wonderful things to discover.

Imagine yourself walking among the trees. Stop to use your senses. What can you see, touch, hear, and smell? Far overhead is the **canopy**, a green ceiling made of the top branches and leaves of the tallest trees. Below the canopy are the leaves and branches of shorter trees. This is the **understory**. Closer to the ground, near enough so that you can touch their leaves, are woody, bushy plants called **shrubs**. On the forest floor, there are wildflowers, ferns, mosses, and the seedlings of trees. If you kneel and dig with your fingers in the fallen leaves, you can sniff the rich scent of damp earth, which is the smell of millions of fungi and microbes. Animals are everywhere. You can hear the singing and buzzing of birds and insects that live in the canopy overhead. You can see squirrels running up and down tree trunks, woodpeckers

Many communities of plants and animals live in the Eastern Forest. Even a rotting log is teeming with life.

The white-tailed deer, at one time endangered by overhunting, is now restored—in some parts, overpopulated—in the Eastern Forest.

hammering on dead branches, small birds picking insects off leaves and bark. From a hollow tree nearby comes the chirp of a tree frog. Turn over a log on the ground, and you may see salamanders, snails, millipedes, and sowbugs. Your footsteps might startle a snake or make a box turtle pull into its shell. After only half an hour, you will discover that trees share the forest with many different kinds of living things.

If we look at one animal of the forest, such as a deer, we can begin to see how the deer and the forest are connected. The deer has an **environment**, which is all the living and nonliving things around it. The **organisms**, or living things, in the deer's environment make up the **biological community**. Members of the biological community can change each other's lives. The deer affects trees by eating their leaves. Trees affect the deer by providing food and giving shelter.

Living and nonliving things in the environment affect each other, too. Living things such as deer and trees can change nonliving things such as soil, air, water, and weather. For example, trees make shade. This changes the air temperature and helps keep soil from losing water. A deer leaves droppings on the ground. Droppings change the mineral content of the soil. Nonliving things in turn affect living ones. Nonliving things such as poor soil, harsh weather, or forest fires drastically change the life of the deer by affecting its food supply or even endangering its life.

All of these connections make life in the forest rather like life in a city. People in a city do business with each other, travel about, live in different places, and have ways of dealing with weather, traffic, and special events. In the forest, different kinds— or **species**—of plants and animals also affect each other, live in certain places, and have their own ways of surviving. The forest "city" is known as an **ecosystem**.

How do we begin to understand a whole ecosystem? The trick is to ask the right questions, like an explorer in an unknown city. A newcomer in a city might ask, "Who are my neighbors? What is the weather like? How does the water taste? Where is the grocery store, the main highway, the gas station, the recycling center? Is there good food here?" An explorer in an ecosystem asks, "What communities live here? Which species can I eat? Which species will try to eat me? Does it rain much? How cold does it get? Is the soil rich? How do materials and energy move around?"

All Together Now

A first look at the biological community—the collection of species— in the Eastern Forest raises new questions. How do these species live together? Do they depend on each other, or do they just live together by chance? The answers are not always clear. For example, some acorns that fall from oak trees are eaten by gray squirrels. Red foxes sometimes catch and eat gray squirrels. In this case, it is easy to see how species depend on each other: these three species—oak trees, gray squirrels, and red foxes—are linked in a **food chain**. A food chain describes feeding relationships in which one organism is eaten by another organism which is, in turn, eaten by a larger organism. Red foxes, the last eaters in this particular chain, are at the top of the food chain.

In other cases, species are linked in a more complicated way. Red squirrels also eat acorns, so they might compete with gray squirrels for food. Hawks and owls might compete with foxes for a share of the red and gray squirrels to feed to their young. Oak trees, red squirrels, gray squirrels, foxes, hawks, and owls can have a great effect on each other. The interaction among all the food chains in a community is called a **food web**.

In still other cases, species do not share foods and do not eat each other, so it is hard to tell whether they need each other for anything. But there may still be links among them. Deer and bluebirds, for example, are not obviously connected in a food chain. But bluebirds eat grasshoppers. Grasshoppers eat plants. Deer eat plants, too. Maybe bluebirds eat the grasshoppers that eat the plants that feed deer. Maybe not. If you study bluebirds, insects, plants, and deer to try to discover links, you may feel like a detective. In fact, you would be a special kind of detective called an **ecologist**, because **ecology** is the study of relationships among species and their environment.

The physical environment of the forest needs to be explored, too. For these explorations, ecologists find out the amounts and times of sun, rain, and snow every year, measure the heights of hills and valley walls, and learn about dramatic events such as hurricanes, floods, and fires.

Features of the physical environment can answer questions about why the forest is found in some places and not in others. Why, for example, does the forest give way to grassland at its western edge? Why does it give way to evergreen forest at its northern edge? The study of the physical environment shows that there is not enough rain at the western edge of the forest to grow trees well, but there is enough rain for the grasses of the prairies. In the north, winters are

Great horned owls hunt animals chiefly at night to get the energy they need.

too long for most trees of the Eastern Forest, but just right for trees of the northern spruce-fir forest.

Vast and Varied

The Eastern Forest is vast. Within it are many different physical environments and different kinds of biological communities. Some regions, such as areas of Indiana and Illinois, have moderate climates that are good for a community of oak and hickory trees. In the coastal plains of the Carolinas, on the other hand, the soil is dry and sandy, and fires are frequent. Here a forest of pines may grow. Along the wet and shifting banks of rivers, there are communities of fast-growing tree species whose seeds can be carried by water. In the sheltered valleys of the southern Appalachian Mountains, a community called the cove forest can be found. In the cooler northern regions, a certain mixture of hardwood and evergreen trees will grow. Examples of these forest communities are shown on the map.

The living things in the forest are not only affected by temperature and weather. They are also affected by whatever is in the soil, water, and air. In some places the soil and water are acidic. That is, they are a little sour, like lemon juice. Some plants grow well in acid soils, but others do not. Soil and water can be rich or poor in minerals such as calcium, phosphorus, and nitrogen, which nourish plants and animals. Some plants do well in poor soils, but others must have rich soils to survive. Soil and water can also contain toxic, or poisonous, metals that are bad for certain plants and animals. If soil gets too wet, some species of plants die because their roots do not get enough oxygen. The air, too, is different from place to place, depending on the amounts of water and the different kinds of dust and gases that it contains. These are known as chemical differences. Detecting the acids, minerals, metals, oxygen, and other materials in the forest helps ecologists understand more about why certain plants and animals live in certain places.

If you wanted to detect chemicals in the forest, what sorts of instruments would you need? You could start with a shovel, and just dig holes to look at soils in different places. New Hampshire soil is likely to be different from Georgia soil, even though both soils are in the Eastern Forest. New Hampshire soil may be dark and damp and full of a mix of rocks, clay, sand, and dead matter. Georgia soil may be pale or red in color, sandy, and dry. These differences give hints about the acidity and mineral content of the soils. With practice, you can begin to predict what forest plants will grow in each soil type.

The Living Engine

Energy flows through an ecosystem in almost the same way that fuel moves through a car engine to produce motion. Living things trap energy. They use it for growth or warmth or movement, and then release it. To follow a tiny trickle of this great flow of energy, start with sunlight on a leaf in the treetops. The leaf traps light energy and uses it to make sugar by the process called **photosynthesis**.

The Eastern Forest

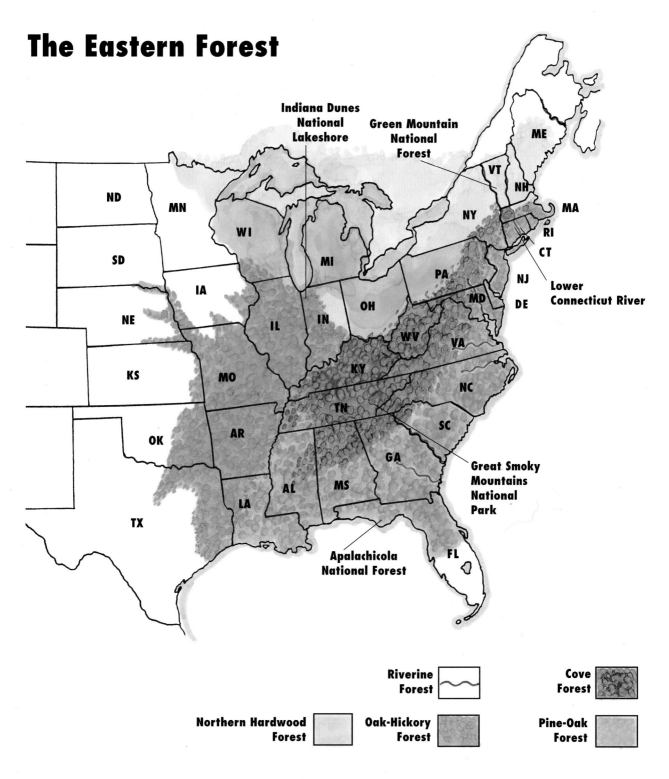

Indiana Dunes
National
Lakeshore

Green Mountain
National
Forest

ME

VT

NH

ND

MN

WI

MI

NY

MA

RI

CT

Lower
Connecticut River

SD

IA

PA

MD

NJ

DE

NE

IL

IN

OH

WV

VA

KS

MO

KY

NC

OK

AR

TN

SC

Great Smoky
Mountains
National
Park

AL

MS

GA

LA

TX

FL

Apalachicola
National Forest

Riverine
Forest

Cove
Forest

Northern Hardwood
Forest

Oak-Hickory
Forest

Pine-Oak
Forest

Several types of Eastern Forest communities may be found across North America from Canada to Florida and from the Mississippi River to the Atlantic Ocean.

This sugar may be stored in a seed such as an acorn. A squirrel that eats the acorn uses part of the energy for growing and part of it as fuel for running around the forest. The squirrel also loses some of the energy in the form of heat and in the form of droppings. Insects and bacteria on the ground take a share of energy from the droppings. An owl might get a small share of the energy if it can catch and eat the squirrel. Sooner or later, all the trapped energy stored in the acorn is used as fuel for the activity of an organism. It is released as heat into the environment, where it is finally lost. No organism can get it back.

Each species in this energy story does a job that has a name. The plant is a **producer** because it uses energy from the sun to produce sugar that animals can use as food. The squirrel is a plant eater, or **primary consumer**. And the owl, which hunts and kills other organisms for food, is a **predator**, or **secondary consumer**. Bacteria, fungi, and other organisms that break down wastes and dead matter are called **decomposers**. Decomposers get a big share of the energy that flows through the Eastern Forest. There are so many of them that their activity raises the temperature of the ground!

Materials move through ecosystems, too, but not on a one-way trip. They can be used over and over by organisms. This process is called cycling. Some of the important materials that cycle in ecosystems are nitrogen, phosphorus, sulfur, potassium, calcium, water, and carbon. You can see how important cycling is by looking at the **carbon cycle**. Carbon in the forest ecosystem is like sugar in a house made of candy; that is, it is part of almost everything. Wood, bark, flowers, fruits, sap, and leaves are all partly made of carbon. Animals eat carbon because it is found in sugar, starch, and other foods.

To see how carbon cycles in the forest ecosystem, let's follow an imaginary particle, or atom, of carbon as it travels. Carbon is found practically everywhere in the bodies of animals. These animals release carbon into the air in the form of **carbon dioxide** (CO_2), a colorless, odorless gas that is a by-product of the energy-making process of organisms. Carbon dioxide in the air is caught

How Carbon Cycles

CO₂

Air

CO₂

Oak tree

CO₂

CO₂

CO₂

CO₂

Owl

Carbon

Wood and
fossil fuels

Carbon

Squirrel

Leaf litter, fungi, microbes

The exchange of carbon between living organisms and the nonliving environment is constantly occurring in the forest.

by a leaf, which uses the carbon from carbon dioxide to make sugar that becomes part of a seed, and then part of a squirrel that eats the seed. Next, it becomes part of the owl that eats the squirrel. The owl later breathes the carbon dioxide back into the air, where a new leaf takes it in to make sugar again. Leaf litter, fungi, and microbes on the forest floor also release carbon dioxide, as does wood when it is burned. The carbon atom cycles through forest organisms again and again, until one day it drifts out of the forest and begins to cycle in some other ecosystem.

The **water cycle** is another basic process in ecosystems. When rain falls, it soaks into the soil. The water keeps soil animals alive. Many creatures in forest soil, such as worms, sowbugs, salamanders, and slugs, would die if the soil dried out too much. Plants also need water from the soil. An oak tree, for example, might soak up as much water in a year as it takes to fill a large swimming pool. Much of the water taken up by plants is released from their leaves as a gas called water vapor. On hot summer afternoons, you can see this vapor far above the trees, as it turns back into tiny drops of fog and forms clouds. Many of these clouds drop rain somewhere else in the forest, so the forest reuses part of its water. Some rain collects on the surface in lakes, ponds, marshes, and swamps, or collects underground as **groundwater**, the water within the earth that supplies wells and springs. Other rain moves quickly in or out of the forest in streams and rivers. Like carbon, water is reused some-where even if it leaves the forest.

Exploring the Eastern Forest means many things. It can mean watching an organism: a living thing such as a deer, a mushroom, a maple tree, or an ant. It can mean seeing **adaptations**, which are the special features and tricks that help organisms survive in a particular environment. It can mean puzzling out a food web, tracking the weather, or finding out how fires and floods affect different places.

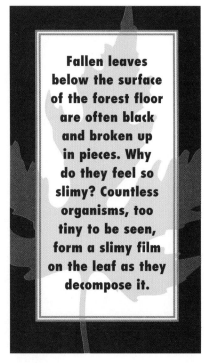

Fallen leaves below the surface of the forest floor are often black and broken up in pieces. Why do they feel so slimy? Countless organisms, too tiny to be seen, form a slimy film on the leaf as they decompose it.

We will explore all of these elements and more by looking closely at special communities within the Eastern Forest: the oak-hickory forest, the southern pine-oak forest, the riverine community, the Appalachian cove forest, and the northern mixed hardwoods. This exploration will also include people. Millions of people live within this vast ecosystem. Whether we happen to be in the city or the country, we have an enormous effect upon the Eastern Forest, just as it, in turn, affects us.

The Great Seed Game

*W*ithin the Eastern Forest ecosystem is a large area called the oak-hickory community. Oak-hickory forests are found in many places, including Massachusetts, Pennsylvania, West Virginia, Indiana, and Illinois. One interesting place to explore is at the northern edge of Indiana, near the shore of Lake Michigan. Here, in a region called the Indiana Dunes, there are many kinds of plant and animal communities, including patches of oak-hickory forest.

Walking into an oak-hickory forest on a summer day, you can hear the calls of blue jays and see gray squirrels overhead. You may taste low-bush blueberries and smell the spicy twigs of sassafras trees. Millions of oak acorns and hickory nuts lie on the forest floor under a carpet of leaves. Some of these tree seeds survive and grow, but most are eaten by animals. In any forest community, there is a balance between the survival of seeds and the survival of seed eaters, but the balancing act is especially interesting here.

Nuts are nutritious. They are packages of energy and other nutrients that a young tree needs to start life. They are also excellent food for an army of animals, including insects, mice, deer, and turkeys.

Oak trees are a major source of hardwood lumber.

A chipmunk proclaims its presence with a loud CHIP!

Perhaps the best-known harvesters of nuts are squirrels, especially chipmunks, fox squirrels, and gray squirrels. These species are true experts at the great oak-hickory seed game.

Squirrels can't live on nuts alone. In spring and summer, few nuts are available. In addition, squirrels may have to compete with large numbers of other squirrels or other species for a share of the crop.

To survive, squirrels need to change what they do from season to season. In spring and summer, they switch to other foods, such as tree flowers, sap, new leaves, insects, and eggs. If nuts are scarce in the fall, squirrels may travel away from home in search of more. If nuts are abundant near home, they may have to chase off other hungry squirrels that have come to take a share. Other species of animals compete for some of the crop, too, but squirrels protect themselves by using special methods of foraging, or food gathering. Gray squirrels, for example, take some seeds right from the treetops, but turkeys and deer have to find nuts that have fallen to the ground.

Who Wins?

With all this nut and acorn eating going on, trees must have ways of saving some of their seeds to grow into new trees. A squirrel might die before digging up all its buried nuts, or lose track of a few, but trees do not have to depend on such luck. Trees, like squirrels, have features that help them win at the seed game. Hickory nuts have thick coats and very hard shells, so many animals find them difficult to eat.

Acorns contain substances called tannins, which taste bitter. (You have tasted tannins yourself if you have ever had a strong cup of tea.) This makes them less desirable as food for squirrels. Tannins also lock up an important nutrient in acorns, making the acorn less nutritious for them. Thus, tannins protect acorns by making them less valuable as food. Some kinds of acorns have lower amounts of tannins, but those acorns give squirrels other problems. Low-tannin acorns are not as rich in calories. They also sprout quickly, which means that burying them to eat later doesn't work as well for the squirrels.

Another form of protection from seed eaters is the change from year to year in the amount of mast, or nuts, that the trees produce. For one reason or another, the oak-hickory forest does not produce the same number of nuts every year. Some oak trees produce acorns only every other year. Others produce large crops every four to ten years and much smaller crops the rest of the time. Sometimes trees produce low numbers of nuts and acorns for several years because of insect damage or bad weather. In such times, the animals that eat the nut crop will probably eat most of the seeds. In other times, known as *mast years,* the right conditions make it possible for trees to produce a huge number of seeds. In those years, there may not be enough animals in the forest to eat all this extra food. As a result, many of the seeds from those years will start to grow into trees.

Seed eaters, in turn, have counterstrategies. Gray squirrels are able to tell the difference between a low-tannin, early-sprouting acorn and a high-tannin, late-sprouting acorn. What

Eat it now or bury it for later? Squirrels make smart choices about what to do with acorns.

good does this do them? It turns out that tannins may be unpleasant to eat, but they do help prevent rotting. If a squirrel buries a high-tannin acorn, the acorn will not sprout or go bad for a long time. The squirrel's strategy, then, is to eat low-tannin acorns right away, and bury the other ones for later in the winter when food is scarce. In years when food is very abundant, gray squirrels can spend less energy traveling or squabbling over territory and more time getting fat and storing nuts. Although they cannot use all the extra food in mast years, they can survive winter in better condition and raise more young in the spring.

By burying nuts, seed-storing animals help maintain and spread the tree species that feed them. Some buried seeds are never dug up again, and they grow into new trees. Also, animals sometimes carry acorns and nuts uphill or into the open before burying them. If some of these seeds grow, the oak-hickory forest will slowly spread into new territory. Overall, the oak-hickory community fares best if the seeds and the seed eaters each win some of the time.

Changing the Rules

Today's oak-hickory forest is quite different from the forest of three hundred years ago. The forest of the past supported many animals that ate hickory nuts and oak acorns, including squirrels, deer, turkeys, bears, and passenger pigeons. As human settlements grew larger and larger, people cleared much of the forest.

In northern Indiana, oak-hickory forest and other forest types were first cleared for farms and homes and later for railroads and industries. The forest as a whole became smaller. Many animals lost their **habitat**—the place that has all the living and nonliving things they need to live and grow. The passenger pigeon became completely extinct, and turkeys and bears disappeared from the region.

Today people are an important part of this forest community. People decide when and where to let the

The meat of passenger pigeons was once a common item for sale in markets. These flocking birds once numbered in the billions, but they were wiped out in the 1800s. The last passenger pigeon, named Martha, died in a zoo in 1914.

The wild turkey has been reintroduced in many parts of the oak-hickory forest.

forest grow or cut it down. There are places where forest habitat is allowed to return. For example, some land that was cleared a hundred years ago for farming is no longer farmed, and forest has started to grow back over the fields.

People have successfully preserved remarkable forest communities that lie along the southern shore of Lake Michigan in northern Indiana. The region that is now Indiana Dunes State Park and Indiana Dunes National Lakeshore was once threatened by industry. Instead of factories, these thousands of acres hold trails through sand dunes, bogs, and forests.

Wild turkeys have been reintroduced in several states by wildlife biologists, and turkeys have begun to live in northern Indiana again. Foresters and landowners are trying to grow healthy oak-hickory forests. These efforts are not only good for wildlife, but good for people, too. Oak and hickory are the best trees for firewood. Centuries ago white oak became the preferred wood of barrel makers, who needed wood that did not allow liquids to seep through. White oak is also one of the best woods for making sturdy furniture.

But oak and hickory trees are still cut down every day to make more space for people. In northern Indiana, some old farms have been covered with forest again, but others have been taken over by houses or shopping malls. Our need for the forest often takes second place to our need for residential and commercial areas. To keep the ecosystem healthy, we must come up with strategies that will help us balance our needs. Like squirrels, we must use the forest, but help it grow, too.

Where It's Drier, There's Fire

There are parts of the Eastern Forest that look like perfect places for a picnic. There are open spaces under the trees and sunny spots where grasses and flowers grow. The air smells of oak and pine bark, and the ground is warm, dry, and sandy. If you were coming here to have lunch, you might even decide to take off your shoes and go barefoot for a while.

Where would you find such a spot? There are some dry pine-oak woods in the Northeast—the New Jersey Pine Barrens, for example. There are jack-pine forests in Michigan. There are pine-oak forests in Illinois. Pine-oak forests also spread through large areas of the South. All of the forests have an important thing in common: they often burn. This may sound like a problem, but in fact these forests are preserved by fire, not destroyed by it.

Fires have brought benefits to the Apalachicola National Forest in Florida, for example. Not all of this forest is dry, but there are some areas where water drains away quickly through the sandy soil. These areas are home to tall, straight, longleaf pine trees and a few oak trees. There is plenty of level open space among the trees, and you can see a long way into the

Strangely enough, without fires,
a forest like this could not
maintain its health.

woods. There are not many shrubs and bushes; instead, the forest floor is covered with tall grass. If something rustles in the grass, it might be a deer coming through or a tortoise plodding by. You may see a flash of black and white and red, high up on a tree trunk—a woodpecker visiting its nest. Signs of life are everywhere.

There are also signs of fire: black charred wood on the ground, gray ashes in the soil, scorched tree trunks, possibly even the smell of smoke. This forest burns often. Fires may occur naturally, such as during thunderstorms, or they may be caused by man. Fires kill off some species and help others. The pine trees in this forest are better at surviving fires than the oak trees are. The seedlings of these pines stay small for several years, hardly poking up above ground level. Meanwhile, they are building big

Fire clears away dead material and creates ashes that fertilize the soil.

healthy roots. Fires may burn the seedling above ground, but most of the seedling is still safe below ground. When the pine is a little older, it suddenly grows very quickly. In just a few years, it becomes taller than the reach of most flames. These features of the pine are useful adaptations.

Where fires are common, pines have an advantage over oak trees. If there were no fires, pines would begin to be replaced by oaks. Also, the grasses that are good at surviving fire would be replaced by other plants such as prickly pear cactus and shrubs. Finally, these other species could take over the forest, replacing the pine community. A whole type of forest community, with many interesting species, would be lost. This is why fires are important at Apalachicola and in many other parts of the Eastern Forest. They keep one type of forest from being taken over by another, and preserve certain kinds of biological communities.

By watching a fire in Apalachicola, we can see how it affects plants, animals, and the cycling of nutrients and carbon. As a fire sweeps through this forest, it leaves ashes and charred wood in its wake. Everything looks dead, but appearances deceive. For one thing, fires here usually burn on the ground and do not destroy the tops of tall trees. For another, most of these plants have some sort of protection against fire, even if they are partly burned by it. They have live roots underground or seeds that will sprout after a fire or tough bark that protects their inner tissues from the heat.

In just a few days, grasses sprout in the black landscape. Fire speeds up the cycling of carbon in the forest. Carbon is locked up as an ingredient in dead wood and dry grass until fire releases it to the air, in the form of carbon dioxide, and into the soil in the form of ash. Then the carbon re-enters the cycle. Carbon dioxide in the air is taken up by green plants, which use it in the process of photosynthesis. Photosynthesis results in sugars, which are food for growing plants. Ash in the soil is good fertilizer for some plants. After a fire, many plants actually grow faster by taking up ash.

Many plants in the pine forest are not destroyed by fires. These plants have adaptations, such as tough barks, that protect them from fires.

Retreat and Return

What about animals? Even though fires do kill animals, they are not the terrible disasters for forest wildlife that you might suspect. Many species are good at surviving fire and even gaining from it. Birds gather insects that are driven out of hiding by fire. Deer can usually outrun the mild ground fires of the southern pine-oak forest. Afterward, they can feast on the fresh green plants that sprout after a fire.

Some animals, such as woodpeckers and squirrels, can simply stay in the treetops above the flames of a ground fire. Other animals escape fire by going underground. In parts of the southern pine-oak forest, animals such as mice, opossums, burrowing owls, snakes, and insects use the burrows dug by gopher tortoises. Some animals actually live in the burrows with the tortoises, while others may just

The gopher tortoise shares its burrows with many other species, who use them to stay cool during hot days.

use the burrows in an emergency. Gopher tortoises are sometimes
called a **keystone species**. A keystone species changes its sur-
roundings in ways that have major effects on other species. The
whole community of living things depends on changes brought about
by the keystone species. Without gopher tortoises in the southern
pine-oak forest, there would be less underground habitat for other
species. Gopher tortoises dig the burrows used by snakes, mice,
and burrowing owls for staying cool on hot days, raising their young,
and hiding from fires.

For people, a forest that burns easily can be a problem. Trees
grow back, but burned houses do not. People now live and work in
dry forests, so forest fires must be controlled. Does this mean having
no fire at all? If there are no fires, more dry leaves and wood pile up
each year. Finally, an accident starts a fire that is very large, hot,
and deadly. In many parts of the Eastern Forest, it is better for forest
managers to set small fires on purpose. They do this every year or
every few years, when conditions are safe and there is not too much
to burn. These "controlled," or "prescribed," burns keep people and
their homes safer. They also preserve habitat for many animals.

The dry and fiery parts of the Eastern Forest are important to
people. In the southern pine-oak forests, huge numbers of trees are
harvested for building and paper making. The forests support deer
and other animals that people hunt for sport or food. People can also
find species in these forests that live nowhere else—species such as
the gopher tortoise and the red-cockaded woodpecker. Apalachicola
National Forest, for example, has the largest number of groups of
red-cockaded woodpeckers in the world.

Success Story

The story of the red-cockaded woodpecker shows how people can
use a forest and share it with wildlife. Today more and more southern forest is being changed into commercial pine plantations, or
tree farms, where people grow large numbers of pine trees to be cut
down for lumber or paper making. As the pine plantations replaced
pine-oak forests, people noticed fewer and fewer red-cockaded
woodpeckers. This was a problem because the woodpeckers were an

*Red-cockaded woodpeckers need
hollow trees for their nests.*

important part of southern pine-oak communities. They ate insects
that ate trees, and their nest holes in tree trunks provided shelter
to other animals.

Why were the woodpeckers disappearing? Wildlife biologists
proved with experiments that the main problem of the red-cockaded
woodpecker in a pine plantation was that it could not find the particular trees it needed. These birds dig their nests in the trunks of tall

pines that have been softened by a fungus that grows on older trees. Old, tall pines were in short supply in these plantations, and the red-cockaded woodpecker—unable to nest—was in danger of dying out. But scientists discovered that the birds would willingly nest in boxes that people had put in the trees for them. The nesting boxes in plantation trees do not hurt the trees, and it may save the red-cockaded woodpecker from **extinction**, or from completely disappearing from the earth.

The case of the red-cockaded woodpecker is a reminder that humans are important to the health of dry forests. The forests are shaped not only by fire, rainfall, and soil, but by living things including ourselves. Grasses and pines, woodpeckers and gopher tortoises—all are important and connected elements of the southern dry forest. Biologists who study wildlife, tree farmers who plant pines, and foresters who light fires are all part of the forest, too.

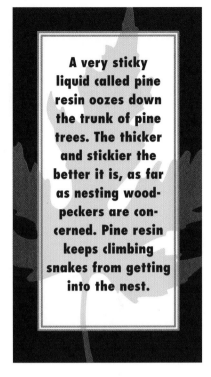

A very sticky liquid called pine resin oozes down the trunk of pine trees. The thicker and stickier the better it is, as far as nesting woodpeckers are concerned. Pine resin keeps climbing snakes from getting into the nest.

Trees Wading Knee-Deep

*O*n the way to the ocean, the waters of Eastern Forest rivers and streams support many living communities. Riverine forests grow along the banks of a river and spread out to the **floodplains**, or the strips of land along the river that are submerged in water. Because a river's edges are always changing, riverine forests face special challenges. The Connecticut River is New England's longest river. It winds through cities, towns, farms, and forests on its way to the ocean at Long Island Sound. The Connecticut River has been used to power factories, enrich the soils of farmlands, provide food, transport goods and people, and—until recently—carry the waste products of human industries. The riverine forest of the lower Connecticut, from Hartford to the ocean, is a fascinating place to explore.

Picture yourself in a canoe along the banks of the lower Connecticut River on a summer morning. As you paddle by a half-sunken log, some bumps suddenly detach themselves and plop into the water— the bumps are turtles that have been resting in the sun. The river is filled with living things, some

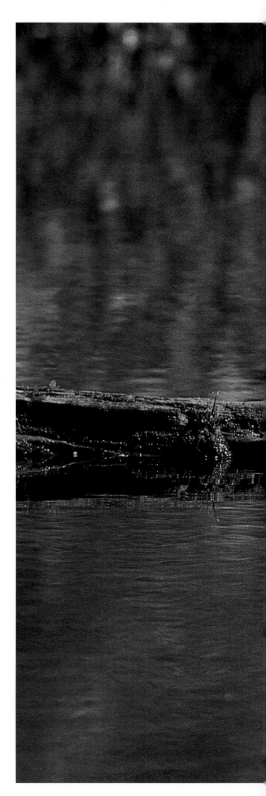

Dead trees that have fallen into the river provide habitat for some of the many living things there.

The osprey, also called a fish hawk, has a wingspan of 5 to 6 feet (1.5 to 1.8 meters) and survives solely on live fish.

destined to become food for others. Brilliantly colored wood ducks feast on tree nuts. Frogs and fish snap at insects. Bank swallows emerge from their holes in the steep banks cut by the river and make wild zigzags as they, too, catch insects. Mink and otters slip in and out of the water, hunting for fish and frogs. Look up and you may see an osprey. The bird stares at the river from its large nest of sticks, high in the branches of a dead tree. If you are lucky, the bird will show you its remarkable fishing skill by making a high-speed dive to grasp a fish in its powerful talons. Ospreys migrate to the lower Connecticut River in spring. They depend on the forest for nesting sites and for the fish that feed them and their young.

Rising and Falling

A river is never exactly the same from one day or one season to the next. In springtime, the lower Connecticut River may rise many feet, until it spills over its banks and floods the surrounding forests, fields, and streets. The high water and swift current may wash soil away from the riverbanks, or move sand from one place and drop it as a new sandbar somewhere else. In summer, the water level drops, leaving dry land where there were wet swamps in spring. In cold winters, large chunks of ice can come floating down the river and tear into the riverbank like bulldozers, knocking down trees and pulling them up by the roots. For at least part of the year, animals can find food or shelter here. When the river rises or falls or freezes, most of these animals can go away for a while if they must. In winter, birds can fly south and turtles can stay at the bottom of the river. But what about the plants? They cannot move out of the river's way.

As you drift along, you can see that even though the riverbank is a risky place for plants to grow, there are plenty of trees: cottonwoods, willows, red maples, and sycamores, to name a few. They are here because the banks of the river have plenty of water and sunshine. Also, when the river level rises in spring and falls again in summer, it leaves behind a layer of fresh mud on the riverbank that helps to fertilize the soil where the trees grow.

Trees of the riverine forest also have adaptations that help them cope with the dangers of the river. Most trees along the Connecticut River can live for days or weeks of standing in floodwater. They can also survive other disruptions. Strong water currents can scoop soil from under a tree, causing the tree to fall over. But some riverside trees, such as willows, have large root systems that help hold soil. Even if they are knocked over, they often keep growing. When floodwaters start to drop, they leave piles of mud or sand everywhere, but cottonwood trees can grow right up through layers of sand that bury them. In addition, cottonwoods and willows grow very quickly. The roots grip the new soil early on, helping to keep the young trees in place.

Many trees grow on the flooded banks of the lower Connecticut River because there is plenty of sunshine and water.

When sheets of ice crash into riverbanks in winter, they strip away the plants and dig up the ground. Once spring arrives, these damaged places are not bare for long. Many riverside trees, such as sycamores and ash trees, have seeds that can travel by water. They float downstream to new habitats, where they sprout, helping a new patch of forest get started.

People and River Forests

The rich soils and beauty of the lower Connecticut River Valley have always drawn people. In many places, the riverine forest has been replaced by lawns, boat docks, houses, roads, and cities. When the river rises, it does not just flood forest anymore. It floods back-yards, buildings, streets, and farmland, too. This can cause very expensive damage and sometimes puts people's lives in danger. We now understand that if riverine forest is allowed to keep growing, it actually protects people's property by slowing down the spreading water. A thick growth of forest also helps to keep soil from washing away into the river.

Inside the "buttonball" fruit of the sycamore are tiny seeds that travel by water.

People have helped ospreys return to the river by building platforms in which they can nest.

People are working to preserve riverine forest— and not just so that homes and businesses will have flood protection. Destruction of these forests means loss of habitat for wildlife. People are recognizing that human activities have an impact on all the living things that depend on the forest, and this impact can be deadly.

Not too long ago, for example, ospreys had disappeared from the lower Connecticut River. They had been eating the fish from waters that contained DDT, a pesticide that was widely sprayed in the United States in the 1950s and 1960s. As a result of the accumulated poisons in their bodies, ospreys—as well as other birds at the top of food chains—were laying eggs with shells that were too thin. Not enough ospreys were hatching. Fortunately, DDT was banned in time for the ospreys to recover.

Every spring, people along the lower Connecticut River welcome the returning ospreys. People even build tall platforms, which the birds use year after year for their nests. The Connecticut River is still a place where you can drift in a canoe, listen to turtles plop from logs, and watch the ospreys go fishing.

Once in a while, a book is written that changes history. Rachel Carson, a biologist, published such a book in 1962. In *The Silent Spring*, she warned of the dangers of DDT and other pesticides. Her landmark book caused a public outcry. People became aware of the tremendous havoc we were wreaking on our fragile ecosystem. DDT was eventually banned and environmental protection laws passed.

Sweet Sugar and Wild Color

The northern parts of the Eastern Forest are full of scents and sounds. You can close your eyes and guess where you are with your nose and ears: in a quiet grove of pine or hemlock trees; near the scented leaves of yellow and black birch; on damp earth beside a rushing stream; or on a thick bed of leaves of maple trees. And if you have come to the forest in autumn, when you open your eyes, the dazzling colors will take your breath away. Climb to a hilltop and look out. You will recognize the trees from miles away by their colors: bright red-orange sugar maples, tan beech trees, golden birches, and emerald green pines. All this variety comes from the mix of species that live in the northern hardwood forest. This forest extends from northern New England and New York west to Minnesota.

A hiker in the northern hardwood forest has plenty to see. Beeches, sugar maples, and yellow birches are three of the most common trees, but there are also pines, hemlocks, oaks, and other species. Plants with odd names live on the forest floor: painted trillium, hairy beardtongue, pink

The brilliant fall display in the northern hardwood forest is a result of a change in temperature and an increase in certain chemicals in the leaves causing the disappearance of chlorophyll.

lady's-slipper, spotted wintergreen, and wild sarsaparilla. A hiker might see fast-moving red squirrels and slow-moving porcupines, or pass by a snowshoe hare that is not moving at all. White-tailed deer often dart across the trail. Moose, bears, and bobcats live in the forest but are more rarely seen.

The seasons bring dramatic changes here. The northern hardwood forest is famous for its colorful fall foliage, its snowy winters, and the spring harvest of maple sap for syrup and sugar. In fact, this forest is one of very few places in the world where people get sugar from trees.

The Year of the Sugar Maple

Change is part of life in these northern regions of the Eastern Forest. A single sugar maple tree offers an example of how living things change with the seasons. In summer, there is plenty of light, warmth, and water. This means that the

As protection from predators, the snowshoe hare's fur changes to white in winter and brown in summer, enabling it to blend with the environment.

maple tree can make food for itself. Green plants use the process called photosynthesis to make their own food. In photosynthesis, the maple tree uses light energy from the sun to combine carbon dioxide (from the air) with water to make sugars. The tree uses some of this food for growing bigger and stores the rest in its tissues. The summer must be long enough and wet enough to allow the maple to do a lot of photosynthesis. The tree needs enough energy to grow flowers, leaves, seeds, and a supply of food to store over winter and use in the early spring. Some of the food it produces is stored in the leaves or under the bark and is also eaten by squirrels, bark beetles, leaf miners, aphids, and many kinds of caterpillars.

In the fall, the tree drops its leaves. This seems like a waste. Those leaves took weeks to grow. The leaves contain trillions of tiny green chemicals called **chloroplasts**, which are the tree's equipment for doing photosynthesis. Why throw them all away? It turns out that this is not really a waste, because photosynthesis slows down in cool weather. Besides, when the leaves freeze, they are damaged. They leak water, and photosynthesis stops completely.

Maples are not like their neighbors, the pines, whose needles survive winter by being fairly dry and watertight. Instead, important components of the leaves are dissolved and flow back into the tree. The tree lets its leaves go, but before the leaves drop, the chloroplasts break down, making the leaves lose their green color. The colors of other chemicals in the leaves are then revealed. The late summer sunlight can also affect the sugars in maple leaves. The result is a colorful autumn display. The leaves of sugar maples blaze with fiery oranges and reds.

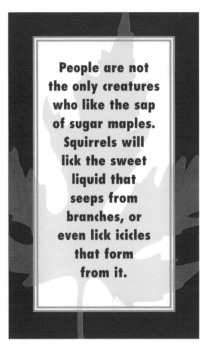

People are not the only creatures who like the sap of sugar maples. Squirrels will lick the sweet liquid that seeps from branches, or even lick icicles that form from it.

People collect the maple's sap from late February through April by boring a hole in the trunk and inserting a metal spout through which sap drips into a container.

In winter, the maple is dormant, which means that many of its life processes are stopped or slowed down. During the long cold months, animals will use the tree in many ways. A moose or porcupine may gnaw on the tree's bark for food. Birds such as chickadees and nuthatches will search the tree for hidden insects. A squirrel might shelter from the wind inside a hollow branch. An owl might use the tree as a good place to watch for mice on a winter night.

When the weather warms in spring, the maple uses its stored sugars to start growing leaves and flowers. Sugars are moved from place to place in the tree's sap. (If you put your ear or a stethoscope against a maple tree in early spring, you can actually hear sap moving in the trunk.) When its new leaves are out and ready to collect sunlight, the maple can once again make food through photosynthesis. Another year and another cycle begins.

Different Species in Different Patches

When a maple seed falls to earth, it joins millions of seeds from other trees, all waiting for a chance to sprout. Which seeds will grow? The answer depends on what has been happening in that part of the forest. In a spot that was an old field a few years earlier, or in a spot that was just logged or burned, the forest will be open

These cedar and hemlock seedlings might have to survive for years in the shade until they are tall enough to reach the sunny forest canopy.

and very sunny. This means that the seeds of white pines, birches, aspens, cherry trees, ash trees, or red maple have a good chance of growing. These species grow quickly in bright light. Once they grow up, they will create a patch of forest that might be too shady for their own seeds to grow. This shady patch of forest, in turn, becomes a good place for the seeds of beech trees, sugar maples, and hemlock trees to sprout. After hundreds of years, the first set of trees will make way for the second set in a process called forest **succession**. The trees that grow first in the bright sun are sometimes called the pioneer species, or early-succession species. The species that grow later on in the shade are sometimes called the climax, or late-succession species.

Luckily for the pines, cherries, and other trees that sprout in the sunshine, there are always spots in the forest that have just been disturbed in some way. Fires happen. Storms blow down portions of forest. Animals, too, can create openings in the forest. Hungry moose and porcupines, for example, strip bark from trees in the winter and kill them. Beavers create whole new habitats by damming streams to make ponds and chewing down the trees around the pond for food. Because of the action of weather, fire, and animals, the northern hardwood forest is always a patchwork of sunny and shady spots, of new and old forest. Since different kinds of trees sprout in the sun and shade, there is always a mixture of tree species in the northern hardwood forest.

People, too, have an effect on the forest. Native Americans hunted here for food and fur, tapped maple trees for sap, and used birch bark for building. European settlers hunted and trapped here as well. They also cut down much of the hardwood for timber. For a while, people cleared the forest for farms, but farming in this region was not easy. The soil was fertile, but summers were short and the ground was full of rocks. By the early 1900s, many farms had been abandoned, and the forest began to grow back.

In the mid-1700s, white pine trees in the American colonies officially belonged to the king of England. Because the pines were made into masts for English sailing ships, taking a tree branded for the king's use was a crime that was severely punished. When the colonies became independent, American shipbuilders used the pines instead.

The new forest is not the same as the old one. The landscape is cut up by roads, farms, towns, ski resorts, and other development. Because of wind patterns, the rain and snow that fall here often contain acids from factories far away. The acids cause aluminum and other metals to dissolve from the soil into ponds and lakes. These metals can poison the living things in those waters and affect all the species that depend on them. In addition, new species of insect pests attack trees. Some arrive through human activities. Asian long-horned beetles, for example, are thought to have been accidentally brought to North America on a container ship from China in the 1980s. The larvae bore deep holes into maple trees, weakening them. Asian long-horned beetles have no natural enemies in the northern hardwood forest.

By building dams and creating ponds, beavers provide habitat for many plants and animals.

To build ski resorts, people carve the forest into fragments.

Still, there are ways in which people are taking better care of this forest than ever before. Timber is cut with greater care than it was in the 1700s and 1800s. Scientists, foresters, and wildlife managers study the forest. They try to predict change and prevent harm.

Every fall, tourists from all over the world come to the northern hardwood forest to gaze at the brilliant colors. The forest provides people with many things, including views of breathtaking beauty.

A Great Treasure of Species

The Eastern Forest covers the Appalachian Mountains like a rumpled green patchwork quilt. Some of the patches on this quilt are forests that also grow elsewhere in eastern North America. But only in the southern Appalachians can visitors explore the complex community called the cove forest.

Coves are sheltered upland valleys, and there are many of them in the southern Appalachians. The Appalachian cove forest is packed with unusually high numbers of species. It has greater **biodiversity**, or numbers of species, than most other forests within the Eastern Forest. The cove forests of Great Smoky Mountains National Park, which spreads across the border of Tennessee and North Carolina, are famous for their biodiversity. They are also famous for their beauty.

The biodiversity of the cove forest is easiest to see on a spring or summer morning. Looking around, you would see that the forest cannot be named for its most common tree species, as the oak-hickory forest can. If you were to describe the cove forest that way, you would have to call it the basswood-silver

Large numbers of salamanders live in the cool moist soil of the Great Smokies.

Appalachian cove forests are found in sheltered valleys covered with numerous plants, such as azaleas and rhododendrons.

bell-tulip tree-buckeye-sugar maple-yellow birch-magnolia-hickory-white ash-hemlock forest! In addition to the trees, varied flowers and ferns cover the forest floor. The air is full of bird songs and the tapping of woodpeckers. A muddy spot might show the tracks of deer, bobcat, raccoon, or bear.

Riches of the Cove Forest

Why do cove forests have so many species? One reason is their excellent climate. Summers are long and mild and wet; winters are cool and fairly short. Plants grow well in these conditions. The plants provide places for animals to live. Their leaves, flowers, fruits, and seeds provide animals with food. In addition, tons and tons of leaves fall to the ground every autumn. This is an enormous supply of food in the form of carbohydrates (sugar, starch, and a woody material called cellulose). These carbohydrates are part of the forest's carbon cycle. The fallen leaves feed a huge community of insects, worms, and other decomposer organisms. All get energy from the food and store some of the carbon in their bodies. These animals are eaten in turn by thousands of birds, salamanders, and other animals. As all these animals use up their stored energy, they breathe carbon back into the air as carbon dioxide. Plants can use it again, and the cycle continues. Meanwhile, decomposed leaves enrich the soil and help new plants to grow.

This trillium flower blooms in early spring when the forest floor is sunny.

Besides the climate, another reason there are many species in the cove forest is that there are plenty of different places to live. Shrubs and grasses grow on hilltops. Pines and oaks live on dry sunny slopes, hemlocks on shady slopes. Buckeye and yellow birch are found in flat valley bottoms. There are streams for fish to live in, and pools among the trees for frogs and salamanders. Birds find food at every level, from the high treetops where vireos pick insects off the leaves, to tree trunks where brown creepers find bark insects, to the forest floor where towhees scratch noisily for seeds.

How Species Live Together

Throughout the Eastern Forest, as in any ecosystem, species are linked in varied ways. Species eat each other, compete with each other, and do each other good. These interactions are especially interesting in the cove forest, because there are so many species using the same area. How do they all get what they need?

To begin with, plants must compete with each other for light. It might seem that tall trees have an advantage over other plants. They catch sunlight far up in the canopy, leaving shorter plants in the shade. But down on the forest floor, there are wildflowers that get light by good timing. Early in the spring, before the trees have sprouted leaves, these wildflowers quickly put out leaves and blossoms. They use the spring sunlight to grow and to store food at high speed until the trees overhead begin to shade them. By early summer, their moment in the sun has gone, but they have made good use of it.

Flowers must be pollinated; that is, the powdery pollen of male flowers must reach female flowers so that a fertilized seed can develop. Many trees have pollen that travels on the wind. Some of it lands in people's noses and makes them sneeze, but most of it reaches other trees. Other plants use different methods. The Appalachian cove forest has whole hillsides covered with bushes of azalea, rhododendron, or mountain laurel. If you stand quietly on one of these hillsides when the bushes are in bloom, you can hear a low hum as thousands of bees forage in the flowers. You will also see flies, moths, and perhaps a hummingbird. All are feeding on the sweet liquid

Using a Berlese Funnel to Find Soil Animals

Animals in forest soil and leaf litter are very small but very abundant, especially where there are plenty of damp wet leaves. One way to get a look at them is to build a Berlese funnel. You will need:

- two large juice cans (32 oz. or larger) and can opener
- a piece of screen about 8 inches square, with ¼- or ⅛-inch mesh openings
- a lamp
- a magnifying glass
- a book on soil animals (helpful but not necessary)

1. Use a can opener to cut both ends out of one of the cans. Cut just one end out of the second can.

2. Put about 1/2 inch of water in the bottom of the second can, and place the can on the floor.

3. Form the screen into a cone shape.

4. Push the screen down through the first can until the point of the cone is at the open bottom of the can, like a paper cup in a dispenser. It should be tight enough inside the can to stay in place, without any gaps between the screen and the sides of the can.

5. Set this can on top of the one on the floor. You may wish to tape them together.

6. Collect about two cups of forest litter from a forest or a park with many trees. Forest litter is the crumbly, moist layer of leaf fragments that lies on the ground under the layer of whole fallen leaves. It is not a good idea to collect from a place where the ground has been covered with bark chips. NEVER collect from a spot that has been sprayed with pesticides.

7. Put the leaf litter gently in the top can so that the dirt rests on the screen.

8. Place the lamp so that its light shines into the top can from less than a foot away.

9. Let the leaf litter dry out under the light for one day. Soil animals should move away from the light and fall through the screen into the water in the can below.

10. Pour your collected soil animals into a dish where you can examine them with the magnifying glass. You can tell what some of them are if you have a book on soil animals. (Look for the subject *Soil Animals* in the library catalog.) If you do not have a book, you can still sort the animals into types and draw sketches of each kind.

11. If there are dissecting microscopes at your school, they are excellent for examining your collection.

12. Try again with another sample of soil. Do you get the same results with soil from different places?

called nectar inside the flowers. They are also getting covered with pollen and bringing it from plant to plant. Thus, species are doing favors for each other, even though they don't realize it. If a mountain laurel is pollinated, then a bee is fed. This sort of relationship between two species is called **mutualism**.

The cove forest is full of birds, such as rose-breasted grosbeaks, bright red summer tanagers, flycatchers, wrens, chickadees, and warblers. If you watch them for a while, you may notice that each species has its own manner of looking for food. Flycatchers perch until they see an insect fly by, then swoop out and grab it in their beaks. Chickadees whack at bark with their bills, looking for insects hiding inside. A warbler might pick insects off leaves. Each has a specialty, so each species is not competing with too many others for food.

If you peer below the moist leaf litter or lift a rotting log, you may see salamanders. These small lizard-shaped animals are an important part of the Appalachian cove forest. Salamanders are really more closely related to frogs than to lizards. They live underground or under leaves or in streams in much of the Eastern Forest. In the Great Smoky Mountains region, there are more kinds of salamanders than in any other spot in the world. Not only that, they probably outweigh all the birds and mammals there! How do they all live together? Some have their own territories. Others compete for habitat. Salamanders are silent creatures, and most are active at night. Their behaviors are hard to study, so there is still much to learn about them.

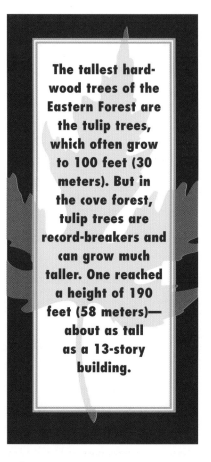

The tallest hardwood trees of the Eastern Forest are the tulip trees, which often grow to 100 feet (30 meters). But in the cove forest, tulip trees are record-breakers and can grow much taller. One reached a height of 190 feet (58 meters)—about as tall as a 13-story building.

Changes in the Cove Forest

People have been in the Appalachian cove forest for centuries. When Native Americans lived in the area, they burned patches of it to grow crops and create places for good nut-bearing trees. When the first European settlers came, they cut some of the trees to use for their own building. These changes were fairly small.

The songs of numerous species of songbirds fill the hillsides of the Appalachian cove forests.

Carolina Chickadee

Kentucky Warbler

Rose-breasted Grosbeak

Red wolves were released in the Great Smoky Mountains National Park in the early 1990s.

By the early part of the twentieth century, lumber companies had taken over much of the land that is now Great Smoky Mountains National Park. Much of the forest was cut down or burned by forest fires. Wild pigs that had been accidentally released were digging up plants, eating bird eggs, and trampling the soil. Insect pests such as gypsy moths and diseases such as chestnut blight began to damage trees. Today air pollutants such as sulfuric acid, nitric acid, and ozone also damage trees. Tourists even trample plants to death!

Luckily, there is good news. Much of the logged forest has grown back, especially in Great Smoky Mountains National Park. Animals that had disappeared are coming back, too. These include the red wolf, the peregrine falcon, the river otter, and a fish called the madtom.

These animals came back with the help of people. Wildlife managers brought otters in from other areas. Red wolves, peregrine falcons, and madtoms were bred in captivity, then carefully released into the forest. Once all these animals were returned to the wild, they were tracked and studied to see how well they adjusted to their new homes. So far, they seem to be surviving. They have become four more reasons to protect the health of the cove forests.

Tomorrow's Forest

The varied forests of the Eastern Forest ecosystem are always changing. Some changes happen suddenly. Fires, floods, and storms can destroy patches of forest. Beavers build dams and turn acres of forest into ponds. Loggers and builders cut down trees. Insects and diseases destroy large numbers of selected tree species.

Other changes occur more slowly. If part of an old forest is cleared, it may be a hundred years, or five hundred, before the same kinds of trees grow on that spot again. It can also take a long time for a small forest to grow bigger. Oak forests, for example, only reach new places one stray acorn at a time. A small oak forest could take centuries to grow a hundred miles wider. If the world's climate gets warmer or cooler, whole forests appear and disappear, but that process takes an extremely long time. As the climate in the eastern United States warmed up after the last ice age, it took about ten thousand years for the Eastern Forest to form.

Hurricanes are one of the many natural forces that change the forest.

Fast or slow, changes are bound to occur. After a fire or hurricane, the forest usually grows back. Wildlife and people return to the forest and begin harvesting its products again. But how much change can a forest withstand? There are limits.

In the last three hundred fifty years, people have brought huge changes to the Eastern Forest. We have cut down or burned large sections. We have brought new species into parts of the forest, such as wild pigs and gypsy moths. These animals have been very destructive to plants and other wildlife. We have also divided the forest into smaller and smaller pieces.

During the last one hundred years, we have burned huge amounts of gasoline, fuel oil, and coal. These pollute the air and water of the forest and weaken or kill forest species. Some air pollutants also trap heat in the atmosphere. This might warm up the world's climate and affect the temperatures and rainfall in the Eastern Forest.

All of these events change the flow of energy and the recycling of materials in the forest ecosystem. A log taken from the forest is a kidnapped chunk of trapped energy and nutrients. A plant sick from pollution cannot use the sun's energy to make enough food for itself and the animals that feed on it.

But so what? We know the forest recovers from natural disasters. If we damage the forest, won't it recover from that, too?

The forest recovers from some of our actions but not all of them. We have cut trees off steep hillsides and let the soil wash away in the rain. Forests cannot grow back if the soil is gone. If we accidentally release a harmful new species into a forest, it can kill off other species before we have time to find a solution. In short, the forest cannot recover if we do too much, too often, and too fast. Some of our mistakes have caused permanent damage.

While we were making these mistakes, we were also learning about how the forest works. A forest is a community of living and nonliving things. Because of the many connections among those things, any change—from reduced numbers of a single plant species to a shift in the amount of minerals in soil—can have far-reaching effects. It may be easy to appreciate forests as resources of wood,

Volunteers work with wildlife managers to build the forests of the future.

wildlife, and recreation. But forests also supply less obvious services, including serving as storage containers for carbon. Trees and their soils contain enormous amounts of carbon. Forests cycle the carbon, so its release into the air as carbon dioxide is controlled. Forests prevent too much carbon dioxide from getting into the earth's atmosphere, where it could make temperatures rise and bring unpredictable changes to land, water, and life.

The management of forest ecosystems requires teams of experts. Foresters try to grow timber for people to use. The goal is to grow healthy trees quickly, cut them carefully, and grow new trees to replace the ones that have been taken. Wildlife managers care for the populations of deer, bears, moose, rabbits, and other game animals. They must decide when there are too few or too many of each species. If there are too few, they may try to create more habitat for them. If there are too many, the forest can be damaged, so wildlife managers look for ways to bring the numbers back down through hunting or other measures. Conservation biologists look after species that are rare, such as the red-cockaded woodpecker, or species that are an important part of an ecosystem, such as the Appalachian salamanders. Other scientists studying the forests include ecologists, soil scientists, and **climatologists**. If you add up all these people, they number in the thousands. But they do not take care of the forest by themselves.

Anyone who cares about forests can try to reduce pollution by using less gas, oil, coal, or insecticide. People can also join organizations and volunteer groups that help to conserve forests. Thousands of trees have been planted, bird boxes put up, harmful plants and insects removed, and tons of trash picked up—all by ordinary people who decided to help out in the woods. People also help forests by supporting reasoned plans about forest use and trying to stop foolish ones.

The future forest will come from choices that everyone makes today. It is important for all of us to treat the Eastern Forest ecosystem with care because it is a valuable treasure of trees, healthy soil, clean water, fresh air, and wildlife. Of course, they are also fascinating places to explore.

Foresters help grow healthy trees.

Tree Troubleshooter

Look closely at trees—in the woods, in a park, or in your neighborhood. You will see that many of them show signs of some problem: an injury, a disease, or a parasite. Here are some telltale symptoms of a tree with a trouble. How many of these can you spot?

1. **Trees with leaves that have holes or ragged edges.** This is usually a sign of insect damage.

2. **Trees with hollow branches or hollow trunks.** These can start as injuries such as when a tree limb snaps off in a snowstorm. The exposed wood can be infected by a fungus, which decays the wood inside the tree. Then woodpeckers or squirrels may dig out the decayed wood and make nest holes.

3. **Leaves that change color during spring or summer.**

    a. Black or brown leaves after a cold snap—these leaves may have been killed suddenly by frost.

    b. Black or dark brown leaves on only one branch—look for an injury on that branch.

    c. Leaves with brown edges—the cause might be drought, high temperature, or sometimes salt poisoning.

    d. Leaves that show fall colors early—this may be a problem in the tree's trunk or roots.

4. **Leaves with spots, bumps, lumps, or large growths.** Many spots and bumps are caused by insects and mites. Lumps and large round growths on leaves may be galls. These are swellings caused by an insect larva living inside the leaf tissue. If you cut the gall open, you may find the larva or see the spot where it lived.

5. **Leaves falling off in summer.** Look at the fallen leaves. Are there twigs attached? If so, something may be chewing through the tree's outer twigs. It could be insects living inside the twigs or squirrels chewing through the twigs to get at flowers, fruits, or seeds. If there are no twigs, and the weather is hot and dry, the problem may be drought.

6. **Trees with crooked trunks.** Sometimes a trunk grows crooked because the tree bent in different directions to get light while it was growing. Sometimes the tip of a growing tree is killed by an insect, and a side branch or two will come around to the top and start growing upward as a new trunk. This last reason is why so many white pines have crooked trunks or double trunks.

7. **Bark stripped or gouged.** Many animals will tear bark from trees. Small torn spots on branches may be from squirrels. Large patches taken off many feet from the ground may be the work of a porcupine. Deer and moose will sometimes strip bark from the lower trunk with their teeth. Bears will scratch tree trunks, and bucks will rub bark off small trees with their antlers. Note: People damage bark, too, by peeling or carving it. This is bad for a tree!

    Do a health check on a stand of trees. Out of every ten trees, how many show signs of some problem? Look in different parts of a forest or park. Does your checkup give the same results everywhere, or are some spots better than others? Compare the health of trees along a highway or busy road with the health of trees deep in the woods. Can you find any clues to show what makes the environment healthy or unhealthy for trees?

Glossary

adaptations the special features and tricks developed by organisms to help them survive in a particular environment. Strong claws and a stiff tail are adaptations that allow the woodpecker to cling to and climb trees, and the shape of its bill is an adaptation for drilling bark and wood.

biodiversity term used to indicate the variety of plants, animals, and other living things in an area.

biological community all of the organisms that live together and interact in a particular environment. The forest is a biological community that includes the populations of all the different plants, animals, and other organisms that live in the forest.

canopy the top layer of a forest formed by the branches and leaves of the tallest trees.

carbon cycle movement of carbon throughout the atmosphere, soil, rock, water, and living organisms on earth.

carbon dioxide a colorless, odorless gas that is a by-product of the energy-making process of organisms.

chloroplasts structures within plant cells that contain the green pigment chlorophyll. Photosynthesis occurs in the chloroplasts.

climatologist a scientist who studies the course or condition of the weather in a place, usually over a period of years.

decomposer an organism that gets its energy by breaking down dead organisms (i.e., by rotting them). Fungi and many types of bacteria are decomposers that feed on dead plants and animals.

ecologist a scientist who studies the relationships among species and their environment.

ecology the study of relationships among species and their environment.

ecosystem the association of living things in a biological community, plus its interaction with the nonliving parts of the environment.

environment all the living and nonliving things that surround an organism and affect its life.

extinction the complete disappearance of a species from the earth.

floodplains the strip of land along a river that is submerged in water.

food chain a term used to describe feeding relationships in which one organism is eaten by another organism, which is, in turn, eaten by a larger organism.

food web a term used to describe the interaction among all the food chains in a community.

groundwater the water within the earth that supplies wells and springs.

habitat the place that has all the living and nonliving things that an organism needs to live and grow. The branches of a tree are a bird's habitat.

keystone species a species that has a large effect on many species in its community or ecosystem. The gopher tortoise is a keystone species because its disappearance from the forest will affect many other species, such as snakes, owls, and mice, which use the tortoise's burrows for shelter.

mutualism a relationship between organisms in which both benefit.

organism a living thing, such as a plant or animal.

photosynthesis the process by which plants and some other organisms that have chlorophyll use light, carbon dioxide, and water to make sugars and other substances.

predator an animal that hunts or kills other animals for food. An owl that eats squirrels is a predator. (See also secondary consumer.)

primary consumer an animal that eats plants. The squirrel is a primary consumer because it eats only plants.

producer an organism (generally a plant) that converts solar energy to chemical energy by photosynthesis.

secondary consumer an animal that feeds on another animal.

shrubs woody, bushy plants that grow close to the ground.

species a group of organisms that closely resemble each other and can interbreed with one another in nature.

succession the process by which a first set of trees in a forest is gradually replaced by another set.

understory the part of the forest just below the canopy that is made up of the leaves and branches of shorter trees.

water cycle process by which water is transformed from vapor in the atmosphere to precipitation upon land and water surfaces and ultimately back into the atmosphere.

Further Exploration

Books

Arnosky, Jim. *Crinkleroot's Guide to Knowing the Trees.* New York: Bradbury Press, 1992.

Behm, Barbara J. *Exploring Forests.* Milwaukee, WI: Gareth Stevens, 1994.

Eastman, John A. *The Book of Forests and Thickets: Trees, Shrubs, and Wildflowers of Eastern Northern America.* Mechanicsburg, PA: Stackpole, 1992.

Goldstein, Natalie. *Restoring Nature: Rebuilding Prairies and Forests.* Chicago, IL: Children's Press, 1994.

Higginson, Mel. *This Earth Is Ours: The Forests.* Vero Beach, FL: Rourke, 1994.

Hirschi, Ron. *Save Our Forests.* New York: Delacorte, 1993.

Lawlor, Elizabeth P. *Discover Nature Close to Home: Things to Know and Things to Do.* Discover Nature Series. Mechanicsburg, PA: Stackpole, 1993.

Leggett, Jeremy. *Operation Earth: Dying Forests.* Tarrytown, NY: Marshall Cavendish, 1991.

Sadler, Tony. *Science and Our Future: Forests and Their Environment.* New York: Cambridge University Press, 1994.

Schoonmaker, Peter K. *Living World: The Living Forest.* Hillside, NJ: Enslow, 1990.

CD-ROM

Earthscape: Exploring Endangered Ecosystems. New York: McGraw-Hill, 1997.

Organizations

National Arbor Day Foundation
100 Arbor Avenue
Nebraska City, NE 68410
(402) 474-5655

Great Smoky Mountains National Park
107 Park Headquarters Road
Gatlinburg, TN 37738
(423) 436-1200

Index

Page numbers for illustrations are in **boldface**.